Contents

1: Opening Time

Stalking Answers	13
Playground	14
Belief in Soap	15
The First Christmas I Remember	16
Opening Time	17
Long Meal	18
Beauty Makes a Baby of Me	19
Nightlight	20
The Bed of Names	22
Hoarse Voice	23
Boy in the Bath	24
Easy Ride, 1955	25
Identity	26
The Hill	27
The Deadly Mantis	28

2: Outline of Thunder

Horses and High Water	31
Hunting Spiders at Night in South Point, Ohio	32
Embarrassed by Flowers	33
Bestiary of Childhood Complaints	34
Shooting the Moon	36
Machine from Animal	37
The Unnaming, 1958	38
Singing to the Fan	39
Boxers' Hands	40
Outline of Thunder	41
Ladder to the Sun	42
Model Fire Building	43
Candlelight	44

The Unfairness of Flying	45
After Prayer Meeting, 1959	46
Tropisms	47
Dreaming the Ghost	48
Dark Drape	49

3: Looking for Life

The Factory of the Body	53
Martial Arts	54
Dancing in the Closet	56
Ode to the Knife in My Ankle	57
Darkness Is for Those Who Can't Stand Shadow	58
Mother Sunbathing	59
Slug Hunting, 1961	61
At Fourteen on the Lake with Grandfather	62
Playing the Piano	63
Looking for Life	65
The Boy Who Fell Through Howell's Mill	66
Reunion	67

4: Nostalgia

One Night	71
Ugly Fun	72
The Sadness of Onions	74
Floating on Lake Vesuvius	75
My Sister's Eye	76
Nostalgia	78
Unrequited Everything	79
Camping at Greenup Locks and Dam	80
Uncle Wind	81
The Quiet Jars	82
Appalachian Gothic	83

5: Some Kind of Pilgrimage

The Mirror	87
Skill to Approach the Rose	88
Winter Gothic	89
Her Hand on the Chili Bowl	90
Birds in the Tops of Winter Trees	91
The Dark One	92
The Wild Ur-Text	93
At Yeats's Grave	94
Undressing Gertrude Stein	95
Last Night Five Young Owls	96
My Neighbor's Great Maple	97
The Exit Sign Over the Body	98
Index of Poem Titles	100
About the Author	103

1.
Opening Time

Stalking Answers

When I was so young my head
    was still full of the fresh fancy
of some foreworld, I would stalk

    the kitchen table to see it
adjusted itself under the load
    of holiday plates and dishes.

I thought it must haunch or kneel
    like a camel at night.
One Thanksgiving, I pounced

    into the living room so hard
I caught the couch off guard. That night,
    I drew red crayon circles around

my bed's legs. If it wandered, while
    I slept, it could find its spot
before daylight. I woke certain

    I'd been carried on its back to where
things graze on what it is they need
    to appear as what we think they are.

Playground

Everything we climbed, spun, or rode
sang hosannas to the coming back,
the sliding down, the dead stop under the sun.

To the playground disciple, the going
up is always worth the coming down.

Mornings I go there before bishop crows
lift off monkey bars, and at evening when last
custodial squirrels scurry away with candy scraps.

Always, I am before and after the squealing
faithful for whom this is heaven on earth.

I come back too much at night to see whether
I can find the ghost of my own youth,
but it won't work without bright sun.

My feet ache like pilgrims
for the exaltation of weightlessness.

In late rain, the flag sleeps against
its dark pole, the slides glaze and slick
with deliverance, all the merry-go-rounds

creaking about freedom, I scarcely recall
the grace of high toys and portal swings.

And gravity, the teacher scolding me
behind the big slide,
never forgets a face or name.

The Quiet Jars
New & Selected Poems
RON HOUCHIN

salmonpoetry

Published in 2013 by
Salmon Poetry
Cliffs of Moher, County Clare, Ireland
Website: www.salmonpoetry.com
Email: info@salmonpoetry.com

Copyright © Ron Houchin, 2013

ISBN 978-1-908836-43-4

All rights reserved. No part of this publication may be reproduced or transmitted in any form or by any means, electronic or mechanical, including photography, recording, or any information storage or retrieval system, without permission in writing from the publisher. The book is sold subject to the condition that it shall not, by way of trade or otherwise, be lent, resold or otherwise circulated without the publisher's prior consent in any form of binding or cover other than that in which it is published and without a similar condition, including this condition, being imposed on the subsequent purchaser.

COVER ARTWORK: © *Daveallenphoto* | *Dreamstime.com*
COVER DESIGN: *Siobhán Hutson*

Printed in Ireland by Sprint Print

For David Reid Dillon

Acknowledgements

Grateful acknowledgment is given to the following journals, publishing houses, chapbooks, and websites where many of these poems were first published, sometimes in earlier versions.

Green's Magazine (Canada); *Infinity Publications*; *Kentucky Poetry Review*; *Kestrel*; *Muse Apprentice Guild* (on-line magazine); *New Delta Review*; *New Infinity Review*; *Now & Then*; *Phantasmagoria*; *Poetry East*; *Poetry in the Park* Chapbook (Columbus, OH); *Poetry Ireland Review*; *Poetry Northwest*; Pudding House Publications: *Greatest Hits Series*; Riverside House Publications; Salmon Publishing, Jessie Lendennie, director, Cliffs of Moher, Ireland; Salmon *Poem of the Week* website; *The Laurel Review*; *The Motif Anthology*; *The Potomac Review*; *The Stinging Fly*; *Willow Springs*; Wind Publications, Charlie Hughes, director, Nicholasville, KY.

Grateful acknowledgement is also due to the publishers of a multiple-author collection and two earlier chapbooks in which several of the poems appeared, often in earlier versions:

Bartley Modern Writers' Series, 1973;
The Courage of Animals, 1991, Infinity Press;
The Falling Boy, 1995, Riverside House.

Thanks to Maurice Manning for the encouragement and idea that led to this collection.

Also, special thanks to Darnell Arnoult, Silas House, Marianne Worthington Mike Mullins, and all the other wonderful teachers and friends from The Appalachian Writers' Workshop, Hindman, KY.

Belief in Soap

At seven, I understood the power in those white bricks
that smelled like cleanness and death.
They kept me safe from the Devil, next to God.

Of course dirt was the world and soap invented by Jesus.
When I sat in the waters of Saturday nights watching
the Ivory float by like a small benevolent barge,

I understood the good Grandma had made me taste.
Truth was harsh and somehow the color of milk.
That which I brought to the rough cloth

was anti-soap. I touched the bar like a base.
Each drop hanging from the faucet showed the world
dangling like fruit no one picked, that dropped into dirt.

The First Christmas I Remember

had nothing to do with bicycles or Lone Ranger
pearl-handled revolvers. It had little to do with anticipating
surly uncles and quarrelsome aunts or a happy little

bearded man. Looking out our front windows,
I watched the street and houses disappear under snow.
At one point, I couldn't see beyond the porch, and the ice

on the windows threatened to do more than frame
the world. That's the way it was in that house.
Any distance from the stoves in December was chilling.

I was forced to go to the Nazarene church and watch the singing
about the appearance of a star. It happened every year.
It was no longer news. I couldn't see the good.

Mostly, I remember waking one night near the 25th
when the wind stopped and I could almost hear
clouds evaporate. I scuffed to the big window

in the freezing front room and rubbed curtain on glass.
It was clear. My feet were stinging, but I opened the door
and tiptoed onto the porch. The air was whiskey, and the sky

had turned to coal. Even the ruts in the road were lost
in the anonymity of deeper snow. But my memory flashes
on the fox standing among blanketed houses.

I've longed to know what he thought he saw
standing there trying to find his forest, his red fur brighter
than snow, like blood on the throat of a lamb.

Opening Time

To avoid kissing my great grandmother's
fuzzy cheek and smelling her fussy perfume,
when she came to visit on Sandusky Road,

I'd scamper to the collie next door
and climb the apple tree above him
as he slept. In the limbs, I was Tarzan

and below me, Simba, my lion.
Whatever I was looking for when I dove
for that low branch was not there.

Solid ground broke my fall
and turned my right arm into lead.
After hospital fear and anesthesia

wore off, something woke in my head.
I carried my slung arm to the sunny west
side of the house and leaned against siding

where a picture of what had happened
lit up my mind like all the lights turned
on in a department store at opening time.

Long Meal

Hoping there might be a fire somewhere in the house
or an air raid siren, I went fishing in the pork slice
at first, happily pulling in bites of chop. The applesauce
swamp in the distance was good for dipping crackers,
for spoonfuls of its own golden tang. And I loved the hot
biscuits defining the day, like clouds, at the edge of the landscape.
I always saved mashed potatoes and peas until last—
a small white mountain and a rounded forest below—
they gagged me while still on the plate.
Whipped and beaten potatoes and hard-looking peas requiring
no teeth upset me, like great-grandma at the end of the table
gumming her slice of Heiners' bread. Near the end of the meal
that I knew was coming, like the dark and the bath, her narrow
eyes judged me as some kind of failure. Looking at it now,
she wasn't wrong. Never mind the potatoes flattened with my fork
into a field of white or the green stars I placed in the upper left
corner. I would dodge the draft and leave my wife and kids.
She tasted it in me. I think the peas and the potatoes did, too.

Beauty Makes a Baby of Me

I can't look at voluptuous mountain
lakes without seeing the tub where my mother,
young and full of new sensuality,
bathed herself and me between her legs.

The waterfall nearby sings and bobs the canoe
like a bar of thin soap. I was too young
to think, but later saw those loaf-sized breasts
and textured nipples in lichen covered rocks.

Had she survived the cancer that ate her lungs,
she would not laugh and shake her head now
to hear this is why I love nature
but always look away. I would hug a tree,

pat a boulder, kiss the mountain's slope,
if I could be certain it would not bring her back.

Nightlight
(1953)

I came to my father's room one night
to tell him dogs were barking
outside my window.

I padded through the womb of the house
to find him lying like a dream
of himself. His side of the bed

was half-familiar like a face
in an old photograph. A yellow wedge-shaped
nightlight was plugged into the wall

above a rack of his pipes. He always hung
them upside down. They appear in memory
like cowled monks praying

for the return of light beneath a triangle moon.
His face hung like a sack of personality
with a gray mustache.

Stranger with his glasses off, he folded
into the cool pillow. I was afraid to wake
him. In such unusual light, he might come-to

having forgotten fatherhood.
It was then I first believed I'd never get
to know him. He was always out ahead of me,

and then he was gone. Only Mother had really
known him. Sixty years on, a dog barks
me out of sleep again, and I pick

my way back to his room, a little less
in the dark, thinking about that nightlight.
He wasn't afraid of the dark and knew

the house like the back of a hand.
That lunar slice of light intimidating his pipes
each night makes him visible again to me.

The Bed of Names
(1953)

Everyone who's ever lived in my other
grandmother's family has slept here
at least once. She reckoned it was my turn,
the winter I was six, the year before she died.

A kind of spongy deck, the bed gave
under my feet. I jumped and slashed
at pillows with my plastic cutlass
on the oldest bed known to me.

As distant lights dissolved over her farm,
shadows widened to overtake their objects.
In the dank air, breaths wreathed her few
cattle below. I settled down into the thick

quilt and blankets to see whether I could
find sleep drifting around in a boat-sized bed.
I felt the carved headboard and fingered over
details of its three-masted schooner.

The night clicked and creaked. No dreams
navigated the ocean. Under my restless turnings,
some rusted spring, like an old first mate,
called the names of a forgotten crew.

Hoarse Voice

Father's back. "After many years
working out west, he's hoarse. Can't
talk much," Mother says.

He sits in his t-shirt at table, munching
Shredded Wheat in milk and apples,
one slow bite at a time.

Wrinkles career across his forehead.
His black eyes watch every move
Mother makes.

His nostrils flare when she switches
the fan on, as if he's sniffing grass fire
and prairie smoke.

Under the table, his thick feet clomp
linoleum. I wear my red kerchief
and cowboy hat.

Boy in the Bath
(1954)

I have a photograph in memory,
a black and white of a six- or seven-year-old
in one of the early molded tubs, the ones
that replaced the clawfoot.

He's sitting with his back to the photographer,
a splash frozen on his left and a large brick
of soap floating on his right. In the background,
the dark tiles have nebulae of splatters.

His head's turned, one eye watching us.
Near his right, washclothed hand, a galaxy
swirls, and a soap dot on the lens almost obscures
his face. The cosmos plays round him. I've seen
this picture pass from album to shoebox.

Everyone thinks I think it's me. I don't care,
brown or red hair, it's not me. Then after years,
no one knows him and wonders who this is
looking over his right shoulder, his eye as black
as the camera's, staring straight into the lens.

All my grandmothers gone, there's no one to ask.
Not even our mother who came home part of each
week, always fatigued from the factory, and remained
quiet in arguments about who came first.

Easy Ride, 1955

When evening holds its autumn breath,
I ride alone through brick alleys.
Houses clicking by and light
through my spokes
make time a slow motion
machine which holds me in place
from brick to brick.
I sit tall among the flat shadows,
and ride easy on the seat
through the half-light.
I look sideways at the brown flowers,
and squint like the sun
at fields full of frowning grass.

Up and down the autumn of my alley,
the colored streamers beneath my grip
breathe and gesture death.
My foxtail waves like a tourist;
we are going somewhere together.
The wind whispers
like intuition at my ears.
All this seems to be—
but look the way the leaves
turn their backs as they fall.

Identity

My grandfather had a membership card
from the American Land Surveyors' Association.
He carried it until it was frayed and soft
on all four edges.
                    It took on the character
of a pet when he'd crease it in the middle
and prop it up on the dash
of each black truck he drove to its death.
He wore a bare place in one corner by pulling
this ID card so often from his shirt pocket.
                                    That shirt,
washed every day or two, had sweat stains
that were always the same,
a wide T down his back.
                        His Levi's
wore so well they glowed skeletally,
an X-ray pattern on each leg.
There was a half-circle of thinned denim
on each hip pocket from sliding along
the truck seat, a small rectangle
where his Zippo lighter lived
                              in the watch
pocket, and a boxy silhouette of blue
in a front pocket for unfiltered Chesterfields.

Each crooked butt hung
for its short lifespan in a permanent
divot of his lip.
                    When I think of him,
I can't see beyond the patterns of wear
wherein he faded.

The Hill

We hugged our Huffys,
like Indian ponies, up the hill.
We ignored the purple, herding clouds.
Things out there could be called in or ignored.
They were simple
in our heads: sun shined, air stirred.
Gravity held it all together.
That it would halt its all-consuming business
if we but walk up this hill,
to give us a ride, was enough
to make our eyes
bug out, hair starch
back and our tongues waggle
out. It was enough to make us
dog-happy. My mouth goes dry
just thinking about it.

The Deadly Mantis

is just ending on TV
again. For the past hour and a half,
she's been eating her way to me.
Still, I am nine.
From the kitchen mother yells it's time
for me to give up Science Fiction
and go to bed.
Instead, I go outside
to punish insect children
for the hours of sleep I'll lose.
The black sky is full of eyes.
Wings flutter and whine around the porch glow.
I grab a moth,
its wings almost cloth.
The powder comes off on my fingertips.
The fine stuff keeps wings soft,
connects it to the air,
and every other living moment. So,
my mother yells again from a grave,
but I won't let the moth go.

2.
Outline of Thunder

Horses and High Water

The first half of December, the earthy waters
stalked up the McMurty fields.
The old man's four horses went to the high corner,
near his house, to stand sad-eyed
and brown as violins.

                When the water
covered the bellies of his tractor and his truck,
he still did nothing, as if disbelief were a sufficient dam.
Above ground like dough, full of dreadmarks, and the horses'
sucking hooves, clouds locked into their docks.
The temperature dropped; sky melted toward Christmas.

                I gave up looking
out the window. The freezing rain still caught
in the horses' hair; ice landed in their lashes.
Each morning there was fresh hay in the highest
part of the lot. It is in such contrasts I hear
the caroling of despair.

                Now, those four horses
have run far from the stable of memory.
The minute hands of snow curried everything
at midnight, saying, Remember,
there is no such thing as lost.

Hunting Spiders at Night in South Point, Ohio

Before he sold out and moved,
Uncle Ben had the whole family
to his farm on Charley Creek Road.
All cousins, our bodies were alike
in ways we couldn't guess.
Scars and cancers not yet visible,
we fanned fireflies into canning jars
and chased each other like ghosts.

Not scary enough for Sue. She knew where
fear trembled, down in the eggplant
garden near the creek. Tiger-faced
things with too many legs hung in trees,
but we thought we knew spiders.
She armed us with flashlights, bigger
and rounder than our eyes.
We filled with darkness like a farm.

The only light was in our hands. Down
the path, tense and tentative as deer,
we walked to the old well-house.
Everything was older than we were
and more rightfully here.
Our slow lights would never have found
the one, large and black as two gloved hands,
that hung across the pathway to the creek,

thrust at us, like a shadow puppet
from the white arms of lightning.

Embarrassed by Flowers
(1957)

The night I saw my cousin Patty bathing in her kitchen
in a galvanized washtub, I was ten and thought of full flowers.
She stood before a mirror watching the water rain
from sponge to her armpit and thigh. I know now she was
about ten pounds past a classical figure, beautiful
and fecund in the dim light; wide, round hips flexing;
a dark triangle of hair pointing down; breasts full
of personality, the color of whipped chocolate.

As she toweled her body, water droplets echoing on tiles,
I saw how her breasts and groin did not work
like the arms, back, head, and legs; but were
shaken by the breeze of her movements, helpless
as if being saved for some secret art.

This was in her house, asleep in the country
except for our two selves. Her children and our other
young cousins slept, crowded into two bedrooms.
I don't remember going back to bed or sleep,
just the great sunflowers that grew, all seeds
and sunrays, around her place. I don't remember
next day if the others played with a box of kittens
or threw rocks at the creek, just my cheeks flushing
when I tried to face the huge blossoms against her fence.

Yesterday, in Columbus's Park of the Roses, I caught
myself blushing again among red, yellow, white,
and pink profusions leaning toward the sun.

Bestiary of Childhood Complaints

1.
In the wide currents of A&P aisles,
gathering produce for Grandpa,
what does cabbage look like uncooked,
out of the bowl? Why aren't mashed potatoes
red? Which came first the orange or *orange*?

2.
At the mirror, wrestling my loose tooth,
I see my mouth become part of a horse's muzzle.
Open, gaping, its tongue neighs
at each movement of twine. No bit, no harness,
just a tiny bridle and the pain of fingers riding hard.

3.
Hanging onto the edge of the closet's top shelf,
my hands turn into lemur paws hauling me
across the crocodile river. I don't understand
the ladder falling away when I lift my feet
or Christmas hiding in the highest corner of the house.

4.
Shooed out the door for church Sunday morning,
hair and ears Brylcreamed back, I'm the rabbit just ahead
of hounding grandparents yapping numbers above
my head. I live by the tic-tock of anyone who reads a dial—
big pictures, loud songs, long sermons. Where's Jesus's Timex?

5.
Dogged by my own tail of shirt, a long johns leg,
and a torn pocket, I have the sense a real tail once
wiggled here, like someone at my back.
Dragging it through sand and water
gives it weight, a mind of gravity. I am alone now.

6.
When I lick my fur, it doesn't change. Like a cat, the sun
licks the world, both go black. Our clean night house
allows no cats, no dogs, no light. I sneak back from the kitchen,
past snoring doors, as Uncle Pete squeaks into my room
to play his game of hiding the mouse.

Shooting the Moon
(1957)

I'd fire arrows and BBs at it
by the score, never thinking what
target they finally found.

What is the moon? I kept asking.
God's shield? The Devil's mirror?
It's not the perfect blister on a black foot

or the green cheese my grandfather grinned
about. In the flat earth of my youth, I believed
only in the plain, not in books.

Trust was straight and close cropped
like my hair. Why couldn't I hit
the crescent, hanging like a banana,

with my .22? The ammo box read,
Range: one mile. How far could it be?
I was ten by Halloween that year

it hung orange as a pumpkin overhead,
God's trick-or-treat mask. I aimed up
and up with the 12 gauge from my uncle's

closet and waited for the wind to die down.
No fluttering leaves in the line of fire.
With the gun butt snug against my shoulder,

I squinted at the shadow of the nose
and squeezed the trigger as I'd been shown.
Light spread over the barrel, each pellet

burned into the sky. Shot sprayed
down round me again, like...spit,
from how far?

Machine from Animal

When I was a kid, I couldn't tell
machine from animal.
The patience of those cars waiting
all night at the curb, like horses
tethered for hours outside saloons,
disturbed my sleep.

In the fields, cows stood chewing
their cuds and shoving out manure.
Our washer or dryer shook
and left a little red pool.
My father wound a grasshopper
up and let it leap into the weeds.
It leaked a little oil in his palm.

Yet, I rode our dog, and teased
our cat, I climbed into our Plymouth
and was driven off to school.
I am still that kind of fool.

The Unnaming, 1958
for Claude Monet

My grandfather, who had a long relationship with beer
and fish, would come back from distant lakes
with one caught carp or catfish
which he'd pour into our clawfoot bathtub.

One night after we'd eaten the thing
that had swum in the drawn water for two days,
he called me to his room where he sat
on his bed listening to hymns on 45s.

'In the Garden' swirled around us.
Cigarette smoke spirited the air.
His gold tooth was gone.
"How do we know what we just ate?" he grinned.

The dark rectangle in his teeth
was an open window. His words
floated out of a haunted house.
I saw his pink tongue hiding in darkness.

His question, the music, the old room—
all were damp and heavy. Suddenly,
everything's name was merely what someone
had put on it. They were like collars.

He warned me Adam was a coward
who tried to tame the world with names.
I slippered off half asleep to the front bedroom
where I believed there was a bed,

and I thought I would sleep.
Back in his room, his Zippo clinked,
The record player clicked.
I supposed he smoked another cigarette.

Singing to the Fan

Though we left the big window fan
on, slicing the air thin, all night,
mornings were still thick and stirless.

I'd hum "Wildwood Flower" into
it's thrumming heart— green
harmony from unruffled trees.

Close enough to conspire,
the way singers breathe as one,
we wove our song.

A warm world fluttered in my face.
I had no love with so sweet a breath
or way of repeating my name.

I close my eyes, now as then,
and there's a dark whirring, a whiff
of mint and mountain laurel,

distant coal smoke, laughter
from the kitchen. I hear
another chorus before it begins.

Boxers' Hands

I long to look at boxers' hands,
white taped for thick gloves.
I picture them crooked and dark where blood
no longer flows to a spaghettied finger
or a hubcapped thumb. When boxers stand,
I think, their hands go naturally clinched.

Their fists may smirk like mouths
they've dug into. Planting bruises,
growing red spouts
make them farmers of other men's faces.

My grandfather sat each winter
watching out the kitchen window.
His right hand held the memory
of hollowing out a Black man's eye.
His left, palm up, counted its fingers
thick as a baby's legs in his lap.
Snow swelled the hills.
Wind abraded the open fields.
Gashes gaped in the thawing pond.
All winter he said his hands ached.

Outline of Thunder

God rolling barrels out the back of a truck
was my grandmother's explanation of thunder.
I think she believed it.

The storm came on running, headlong,
like a maniac down the hill
to the next victim's house.

Grandmother flicked off the TV
before the rumble got to hill bottom.
She knew lightning could travel

power lines and blow up in the living room.
I sat on the couch hugging my knees
and pictured lightning bouncing through walls

like a glowing basketball.
A sort of unscheduled commercial for God
rolled on overhead.

She closed windows through the house
then pulled the Bible onto her lap.
Sky the color of turnips split in two.

The terror of night intruding into day was,
for her, like war. Darkness dropped bombs
on both sides of the narrow house.

She twisted her hair into a helmet
then patted plague, death, murder
in the black default of her god on her lap.

Her life flashed black and white,
hours and years flickering in a dark room,
a lone life with remnants and brittle frames

of the dead. I watched her marmoreal
face listening to the past, to the lonely
ransacking of sky and mind.

Ladder to the Sun

I had no intention of remaining on earth
after school. Mother wasn't home yet, and I loved
September's slow light and spotted leaves.
Already into glass-globe days,
the sun experimented with different intensities.

The two-story ladder lay behind the house
as if it were tired of being wood. Where sun
touched it, came warmth, and cool dampness
where grass held on. Young enough to think
a bright ball hovered just above the house,

its smiley face hidden by glare, I hand-walked
the parallel arms up and leaned them on leafy gutter.
Each rung I climbed, light grew, until I gripped
tiles at roof's edge. From there, I smelled leaves
piled for future burning. I saw sycamores lining

the backyard, the small chicken coop lodged
in lot corner, the height and distance of everything:
Firemen washing the red, glistening ladder truck
and patting it dry in front of the station.
Like a friend, my sun-heated shirt encouraged

at my back. A giant gold disk enflamed the blood
behind my eyes. I had made it: one step from rooftop
and the heart of September. Up here, unblocked
by houses, the siren's sudden whoop then wheeze
blinded my ears, slapping my balance.

All stories flew out from ladder and wall.
I dropped, the earth disappearing, babbling
from a crumbling tower; my fall turned
into jump for leaves piled just right,
onto short lives spun by delight.

Model Fire Building

When I was young enough
to want to embrace fields,
talk to flame and dance around trees,
I'd climb to a cave used by cattle.
The floor was cratered and pocked
from their heavy hoof work.
The ceiling had the texture of an unshaved cheek.
I played there in the thin darkness
and built small fires to keep the big bodies out.
After several of my visits, the cattle would amble
away as I gathered wood.
There among the ammonia smells
and sandstone skins, I'd crouch
on a pissing-rock and stack twigs.
Where some boys built model trains or cars,
I collected cottonwood, locust, maple
in the thinnest samples I could find.
I prepared them, pared them, shaved them,
and added flame from a rebuilt Zippo.
I kindled it down to tiny
hot presences crackling against the dark.

Candlelight

After the power went off,
a dinner candle from the drawer
showed me a place that hadn't existed
seconds before. I walked
the hall between windows, between
shadow-puppeted walls. Lightning flashed
on both sides of thunder, and the flame
shook. This bit of nature squirming
in my hand was my light-hostage
in the storm. And Florida lightning,
the mafia of lightning, would kill
me and my whole family,
wherever they were, for return
of this one hundred millionth
descendant of first flame.

In the nickelodeon of night,
all fire knew the nature of the
darkness from which it flashed.
I wished my grandfather were home
to tongue his yellow teeth,
light a big match,
suck it into his cigar,
and tell me to watch the show.
I sat at the top of the stairs
staring at the candle
that wore itself down as its other
self formed. In the saucer,
the flame guttered into a spread
of diluted green. A tiny piece of wick
fell into soft remains. Lights came on
in anticlimax and darkness leveled
out. A mosquito found my arm
and its own smack of thunder.

The Unfairness of Flying

Monday, to encourage the growth of wings,
I taped butterflies to my back.
I jumped from rooftops and swings

to make the need real,
folded paper airplanes all naptime
and tied them to my heel.

Tuesday, I strung June bugs in my hair,
little engines buzzed my ears;
blue ribbons trimmed the air.

Wednesday, I had my feet all over trees,
walked long limbs to the end.
With my stick, I lectured bees.

Thursday, slept on my stomach, arms outspread,
bounced on furniture all around,
and broke the springs in my bed.

Friday, picking up dead crows in the park,
I hung them like wind chimes on the porch.
All night my window curtains flew in the dark.

After church and Sunday school picnic, ferlies
faded, voices murmured, nothing joyful filled the air,
men, like leaves, lay under trees.

Monday, at recess, I watched others play.
The bell rang, swings quit squeaking,
birds preening in dust puddles fluttered away.

I popped my lunch bag. Something red
zipped from the hedge. It seems to me
most things fly in fear and dread.

(Ferlies, Appalachian English, from Middle English ferly, strange, wonderful,
unexpected—Walter Skeat's *Glossary of Tudor and Stuart Words*, 1914)

After Prayer Meeting, 1959

At twelve, just back from the Nazarene
church, I burned trash by the fence,

singeing my hair and eyebrows
at the barrel in the alley.

My fingers teased one-seventh
the heat of Hell.

Windows in the neighborhood
blazed up with evening,

and I wondered who stands stirring
the burnt wrappers and tins

of souls each twilight over the dark
rim of the world.

Tropisms

When Mary Igo turned the high beams
of her sixth-grade smile on me,
it was the first time I understood
the laws of attraction— all of Mr. Thomas's
efforts in science notwithstanding.

Even though I knew the grasses
were being pulled inexorably toward
the sun they'd never get close to,
and the planets themselves grumbled
and shouldered dissimilarities out of their way,
something opposite in my hydrogen sought hers.

Even though I felt a new Disneyesque bond
with all those differences out there
and believed it all came down to a big bang
and the irregular arrangement of electrons,
there was Mary's smile, her blond hair,
and her always-clean catwoman glasses.

But for several months, well past Christmas,
all my atoms resisted her Eves,
until enough testosterone circulated;
then something barely significant but
omnipresent in my mind leaned toward her,
like a philodendron in a bright window.

Dreaming the Ghost

The light thunder of grandfather's voice
    prays for new surveying work between puffs
        on Old Golds. My head clearing,

I remember the body-length stretch
    of land he's measured at Spring
        Hill Cemetery since last Thursday.

A nattering flame flushes light
    up the hallway to where I sleep,
        thick covered till he comes

to my bed to stare. Late clink of Zippo,
    pop of bad knee wake me to tobacco
        and smoke apparitions at the door.

Swirls in room darkness threaten to take
    my thoughts, and grief to dream me
        a wet morning that felt

like night. No matter how old I get, I hear him
    rise from his mahogany bed to hum
        "In the Garden" from the next room.

Dark Drape

Any cap or hat landing on beds, my grandmother, mother,
or sister would knock across the room, lest nightmares
and stillbirths take the family.

A jackknife opened by me could not be closed
by anyone else. In a cup, ink pens must be stood
points down and pencils points up
or words might change on the way to paper.

Only an idiot stored brooms in the closet bristles up.
Gods are particular about what gestures heavenward
or lands on beds.

I stepped on sidewalk cracks to and from school
when my cowboy hat and ball caps were strewn about my room,
my open knife flung into the backyard, and my pens stuck
in the ceiling, as if sucked up for punishment.

A god stood over the houses of each neighborhood
and followed believers everywhere, especially to church,
watching how they wore their belts, carried change
and chewed gum.

The only superstition I liked was the absence of fire and light
on Sundays. The house stayed dark but for opened curtains.
Food was served cold from cans.
A dark drape hooded the TV for Dad's "Gunsmoke."

3.
Looking for Life

The Factory of the Body

The first school encyclopedia I remember taking home was *THE BOOK OF KNOWLEDGE* which sported several black and white illustrations in a section "The Factory of the Body." Each organ walled in its own area had tiny, white, featureless men pulling levers and pushing cogwheels in the head and torso.

The groin, where my preteen eyes darted, was dark, as if its bulbs had burnt out, as if installing outlets had somehow been forgotten, and all extension cords were too short to reach such a remote zone.

Part of our shadowy fate as children of industrial workers was to understand these anonymous laborers punching the clock and manufacturing life for us. Owners of our own factory of body, we felt the weight of responsibility for production and safety of all our departments. Health was a matter of maintenance and labor relations.

My stepfather, a life-long steelworker, assured me early union meetings were often held in such unlit regions. My imagination, not believing in neutered factories, worked on, hard-hatted by ignorance, contracted in dark wonder.

Martial Arts

> *"...and it's possible to paralyze*
> *a giant locomotive if you know*
> *exactly where to put your finger."*
>   DAVID HAWKINS
>   *POWER vs. FORCE*

She grabbed my wrist, her thumbs
in a spot I remember clearly on the body chart
                        of pain.
Her eyes burned, not into mine
but beyond, to a point past this event,
                where it would lie in her stories
of amusing triumphs.

Her elfin size had nothing to do with it.
Her blanket-robe was loose and full,
proper to the event,
                   one of those
spontaneous games mixing
tag and Dracula—
the person *it* was the ferocious count
who threw cape about victim
                     and pulled him to the ground.

She had extra strength for the role,
            never having heard from four brothers
how big boys can't be thrown by girls.

When caught,
            I hacked at her ribs
rather than go down. Holding my shoulders
by the sweatshirt, she spun me
            in a circle, which turned into

a dance maniacal.
                      For two seconds,
I was her weightless partner.

Over in the evening field,
an impromptu football game
halted
at the gun crack,
                      on the only
boulder in the Commons, of my right femur.

Dancing in the Closet

I had to whirl. I had to be quiet.
Saturated and wrapped in a thick towel,
I hobbled from shower to closet—
Mother, stepfather, sister downstairs.

For the darkness and the leg weakened
by three previous breaks, I slunk into
the tiny chamber to celebrate and shout
things forgotten, things regained:

Little room where raincoats
and house robes hung like ghosts,
I can run again!

A fit of well being overtaking me
on the way home from West Junior High,
I'd run two blocks, graceless,
but with speed against a small dog—
the first time in three years.

Among seasonal bonnets and all-but-forgotten
hats that used our hair like screw
threads to hold themselves on, I felt nothing
holding me and no thing
keeping me back.

I was almost in a box but free
to slip gravity, free to return to Poe
and Lovecraft or run in the cemetery, healthy
enough to re-open the romance of the grave.

I kicked the shoes and boxes aside
and spun, legs crossing and stomping, crossing
and stomping as fast as night wind.
Life was near and death, jealous again.

Ode to the Knife in My Ankle

I know how you got there,
flung back at me in anger,
when our game of mumblety-peg
got out of hand.
           Your sharp tip
disappeared like the end
of a black exclamation point
into the vein that snakes
across the rock of my ankle bone.
              I started it,
tossing your mean-spirited point
into Jerry's retreating neck.
            And he ran up
and gave you back,
in the next instant.
       One surprise: his throw hooking,
like a girl's; another, my insides
running out.
          Writer in red
on the tablet of my leg, I know
I deserved your message.
              What are you now
in this memory?
           Scar before car thefts
and gang fights to come,
reproach for not joining the circus
and learn a real knife trick,
            flying fish trying
to return to the lost lake of childhood?

Jerry had little taste for the way
daggers get around,
get stuck, stab, or thrown.
              I thumb your edge
like the bottom of a page. Welcome back.

Darkness Is for Those Who Can't Stand Shadow

When my cowboy life comes back,
and I can't sleep in my bed,
I wrap an image of prairie
around me, like a towel.

I put on some exhausted clothes,
dig out my Boy Scout bedroll
and cook kit, and set up Minnesota
in the closet on top of my shoes.

With the door shut, the closet has no shadows.
In the clear dark, there are no coat sleeves
in my face and no wall at my elbows,
only dark prairie as far as I can think.

Somewhere on the next hill, wind ruffles a buffalo's fur.
Over the wet grasses, it enters my nose.
There is dirt in both of my socks,
and, at last, I'm sleeping on burs.

Mother Sunbathing

She held court from a bench of rays,
as if lying naked, bright
in sunlight on her day off was
the only thing worth doing.

With L&M's, thin silver lighter,
Coppertone, and mug of Coke,
she lay in exile for beauty.

I was not allowed in the back
garden except for emergencies
or warning of stranger's approach.

She had found the geometric
center of privacy in our
yard. The screen door screeched alarm if
opened, our two small trees, one shrub
and a continuous hedge couched
and blocked her from every

angle but one. I came home that
way one day, through alley then
garage. Rainy but clearing, sun
peeped out every other minute.
Where she lay in striped chaise lounge,

her breasts, like the source
of my mythology, were
golden water poured from a high
amphora across her chest.

Forgetting her wealth, for a moment,
she sprang up to scold then folded
her arms into a makeshift halter.

I had no words for telling her
I loved her working the living
equipment of her skin with water,
oils, and light as if it were

furniture where someone might
comfortably live, a place where
life might begin. She would not

approve this observation, unless,
now, she lies somewhere other
than Ridge Lawn Cemetery, more
in enlightenment than in light.

Slug Hunting, 1961

Summer night, air like a bathroom
shower, my t-shirt clings to my back.
Number 10 coffee cans and rags snatched up,
we trot past the bait shop
where we'll sell night produce
after rolling logs and flipping fat stones
in backyards . . . a nickel a slug,
good enough against squirming canfuls
of nightmare and slimy hands.
By midnight, the town's a bedroom.
We tiptoe through each gate and breezeway.
In our last yard, morning
glories overgrow the fence.
Sweeping our sleepy flashlights,
we separate. Charlie,
near black windows,
tips a birdbath and slides a stone bench.
At the alley fence, I pry up old lumber.
Lost in the glory of slug scum—
they lie like alien invaders surprised in the act
of disappearing— I don't see the night cruiser
release its two officers, flashlights cocked,
in time to rasp to Charlie, "Get down."
The first blast hits him in the back.
I pop up from the fence, the tall cop's hand
goes to his holster. Explaining
our permission does no good.
At the front door, apologizing
to the stunned new tenant and her daughter,
Charlie and I stifle laughs watching an escaped slug
undulate along the short officer's gun belt.

At Fourteen on the Lake
with Grandfather

Standing in the boat on a clear day at
Beach Fork is like standing on the great
lip of the world. I know something's
down there as tackle *ploinks* into the water.

Before grandfather can say, "Reel her
in. Don't give her too much line,"
I think of the fish as *she*. She is
swallowing my offering,

and I am lifting her from water
into a world where she cannot live.
Now, I've got to get her into the boat,
close to me, to be held in the sun

and air of my fantasy.
She smells like the deep mystery of
the world's insides. She is *all*
things bright and provocative.

I look into her face thinking
this will make a great memory,
as if we are alone and I am capable
of more than one kind of love.

Playing the Piano

Like a horse, it had been led in
beside long planks of sunlight.

When I was done with it,
years later, my stepfather
wanted the piano out of the house,
out of my room, the once-garage.

All the pedals stuck, three keys
stayed down when plunked,
and mildew had eaten the varnish
off one flank.

The fall opened by screwdriver.
The lid would not lift.

I was handed an ax to put the old
Campbell out of its misery.

First stroke took the front leg off;
body clamored to the cement floor.
My grip
raged at the nights of not learning "Nocturne."

I chopped away through screeching
rosewood and black and white keys.
An old secret, its harp lay sprung and forlorn.
I expected to find something occult coiled among

the wires and metal frame. I chopped
it into bell-shaped pieces
and carried music out one clang at a time.

I barely fitted them through the new door.
From the center of the wreckage, I hacked at a heart

that pumped out notes connected to light
the way bad children dissect
cats in alleys expecting
the core of death to purr god.

Looking for Life

I remember looking straight into the gash
something sharp in the trash had cut in my palm
when I pushed the bag down into the tight barrel.

That squiggly stuff in the soft tissue
between forefinger and thumb, I thought
was life, until I turned over the largest stone

I could tumble in the backyard. All those
white grubs and pressed, naked earth reminded
me of the stuff inside my hand. Where

was life hiding? My tenth grade
biology teacher had started it, making us
look at life, which I translated as *for life*.

My little camera caught dead things close up,
as if life leaked out like air from a lost balloon.
I watched cats and dogs. Their teeth and tongues

spoke of life, unlike the gibberish of people.
I agreed to go to church the next Sunday, in case
life hid there. I hadn't been, for long sermons

of time. No dice, just light bouncing
from the money, Sis and I tried to count.
Then, I thought I'd found it in you, in you

and your wet groin. The musk of hair,
fluid and mild bacteria. Why wouldn't life
be where life begins. We made a fun soup

that stuck to our hands. We grinned.
When I walked you home, you said,
"Tomorrow, we dissect pigs."

The Boy Who Fell Through Howell's Mill

left behind the hostile spikes and edges
of broken mill pipes we stamped among
waiting our turns at holding his hand trapped and
freezing beneath the mill floor in Mud River.

He is survived by our memory of the taste
of rusting iron where we wiped
our snotty faces on frozen sleeves.
He left us the smell of cold stone.

Bequeathed to us was the time still ticking
in our flesh as we held onto his
under ice water, the strangling gargle of falls
falling and holding under all that plunged there.

He left us that running skin of water and
gray skull of stone beneath, for lifetimes.
He gave us our grief turning into holes
in the cement floor where huge millwheels

were removed like vital parts pulled
from a giant heart. Our dancing cries had him
in them. But the first thing he left us
was the cold sting of understanding that this

is the way the world is sometimes—
that rank tree root we hung upside down
trying to pull up had never been the hard arm of
the drowning boy caught in the undertow.

Reunion

The body's a stranger
I introduce to every body
I meet. This family is a group
of minds that looks out at strangers,
looking for the familiar one inside.

We meet again, after years, almost knowing
each other at the picnic in the park.
We are like the chicken
on the tables in plates—
together at awkward angles.

The body speaks its own language,
talking of time in hieroglyphs
around the eyes, wonder in the ridges
of the forehead. It trembles when
the steak knife licks its thumb.

Before Aunt Hazel, I sit leaning
forward like a preacher. I see my
hands, below them my shoes.
I have been here for hours, so they
are family hands, family feet in
store-bought shoes.

I'm walking again,
doing what I think a cousin here,
an uncle there, a nephew, a father,
a husband, a grandson, a son, should do.
The body walks among the cars
that have changed less
than the ones who drive them.

At the shelter toilet, I let the body's
water out. I want to go with it.
A distant cousin and a nephew
are making their moustaches and smiles
match in the mirror,
but I can't look up from the soap
to the mirror. I don't want
to see the stranger that's always
looking back at times like these.

4.
Nostalgia

One Night

I wake in the dark,
looking at a window.
I try to recall where I am,
in which house,
at what point in my life,
what window that is.
Almost pleasure,
almost panic, this is
like floating in a night river.

I see the skeleton of a bookcase,
the brocade of a few
dark trees, a star, and the drift
of a tiny red light across the sky.
I know if I stand, memory
will rush in and rescue confusion,
but for now I want to
ride out the uncertainty
of whether my parents are
down the hall or dead.

I feel the zing of consciousness
so I am still somewhere
in the universe. In the quiet,
I trace initials that could be mine
on the night air.
I don't want to remember
whether I have children.
This could be a dream just ending.

But better than dream is
this moment, being lost
in a room, not knowing
where the light is.
I am weightless, for a second,
not sensing whether I am
a man or a woman,
whether needles or leaves
sleep in my groin.

Ugly Fun

On the porch before
all the stars have come out
to breathe the evening,
I am spitting tobacco juice
on small frogs that try
to hop up three steps
to the porch after rain
and dampness have all but
left the cement stairs.

I spit a circle of brown
puddles around the smallest
frog scoping out the porch.

I expect to see a small flag
rise over the ridge of the top
step, as if the advance guard
is ready to take up defensive
positions for a division
of army frogs, and I have
the lead scout trapped in
a circle of noxious chemical.

I am nine and the Korean Conflict
is just over. In less than a decade,
I will be asked to go to Vietnam
and drop napalm on villagers.

I won't do it. I would like
to say it is partially
because I used up my portion
of cruelty on three or four
tiny frogs. It is not that,
for I have begun

to change from a running villager
to a helicopter pilot
in my own family war.

And I know my love of ugly fun
just grew as my sister tripped out
onto the dark porch to show
me her new Snow White pajamas.

The Sadness of Onions

When her two grown sons were home for long
and fighting in the yard or gone
some months bad-check writing
in their father's name, my grandmother
would sit in her dull kitchen crying.
Every time I asked her what the matter was,
she'd say it's from cutting onions,
invisible ones. I don't know how long

I believed tears from all unseen
injuries were the sadness locked inside
white vegetables. I don't know how long
I thought, in my family, the women
just like onions
so much more than do the men.

Floating on Lake Vesuvius
(1968, Wayne National Forest)

Peace was a word that surfaced a lot.
It was near summer's end, and I had no idea
where the center of this meandering water was.

I wondered why everything couldn't just float.
Why did crows have to work hard to cross the sky?
They couldn't glide on the pulling

of the horizon? I wanted our family car
to be able to coast downhill all the way home.
Everything was drawn, urged along, so why not

let the march take us along?
Floating there, wherever I was, drifting
the third week back into school,

I marveled that I didn't just peel off
the planet, like a parking sticker or fall
to the bottom of the lake like a wet leaf.

But I arched my back, the way water liked
and it held me in the soft ballet of floating.
Just as on the roof of the barn,

and the college dorm building, I lay
where night sky and salt stars filled my eyes,
the world a harder place to hold onto then.

My Sister's Eye

When I read Cooper and decided I was the last
of my tribe, I whittled my spears down
in the cave made by the gooseberry bush.
My sister came out wanting me to dance.
American Bandstand was on again. She couldn't
have guessed I was in my Indian mode,
plotting the destruction of the White Race.
While I charred the wooden points
in a small fire, and the smoke disappeared
among the leaves and limbs above,
she ran up with a double handful
of gooseberries and sandstones and tossed
them at me and the fire. If I tell you
I smeared the berries into war paint,
it is my spear sticking from her eye
I see. When I speak of the stones exploding
in the flames, it is the squish
of the burnt point entering her head
that I hear. If I mention I ran off
to the reservation of my room, I see
her dance of horror down in the yard.

After four decades, we don't talk about it.
I wonder if she sees her half of the world
as a place where mad brothers in buckskin
knock out half the light. If I could
track us back to that afternoon, I'd
throw my shirt over the fire
and send up smoke signals to those badlands
about what it's like to live with
a vision when the vision turns renegade.
I'd let the message waft into the still sky
that it all had something to do with the way
our grandparents saw only her, and how

Father was gone and Mother had moved
to the other side of town.
How I felt massacred in that old house;
how blindness taught me to see only
Hurons on the horizon.
How all these years
I have made excuses
useless as beads.

Nostalgia

Coming back home after weeks
at another's house, I long
to see my things. My favorite
chair waiting like a horse
in a dark stall. My old table
with every word I ever
scribbled on its dull palimpsest.

Photographs of the place
I just left waving hello
from the old sunshine
of my walls.

Little appliances
grazing on stillness and silence
in the kitchen lift their electric heads
the instant I touch their switches,
and I know I've disturbed the peace
in some kind of museum.

Nothing can
take me higher in the house
of homesickness than seeing
the change I dropped on
the bedroom floor still there.

Unrequited Everything

The only satisfying day I can remember
was one autumn afternoon in a cemetery.
I can't recall who died, but several of us
were there, like wet crows standing
around watching what had fallen.
Rain dripped from iced twigs.

The grain of tombstones filled
black and white air, nameless
in the calendar and invisible
on the clock. Everything showed its parts,
its pieces. The open sod steamed.

Funeral home limos lined the street—
barges for a cargo of anonymous grief.
We seemed to think in slow motion. I don't
know whether we walked in clinging grass talking
about the deceased or played with the hollow ache
of loss, each like a six-year-old with a new scar.

The day hugged emptiness, the familial
sound of raw rain, a close echo of metal
and sighs. No sun distracted from the mystery
of coming darkness. A name
hung like an unanswered prayer.

Camping at Greenup Locks and Dam

This river has only a throat.
It practices Germanic vowels through
the concrete fluting of the dam.
We think we are fishing in gray-green water
at evening, Zebco lines pissing from our hands
past the swollen torsos of locust and cottonwood
frozen there like last month's murdered.

The wind tries to unturban the towel from
your washed hair and nothing
wants to be where it is.
God forbid either of us catch a fish
and try to reckon its origin.
As it grows late for a Sunday, I question
our Mondays and the machine that brought us here.

And I have no patience
for these boulders thrown about
like pocket change from the moon. I watch you
crouching at the end of the dock trying to think
through a confusion of filament and I want to lick
the sand from that biggest rock
for its understanding of time.

Uncle Wind

Like a drunk raging against the return
of sobriety,
wind stumbles between the houses

rattling each window with
a fat elbow.

At the back door, his hands grow numb
from staggering in

the cold, so he fumbles
the knob then shoulders wood
and moans,

but I am freezing at this window
and remember he changes

with drink. So the dilemma of
childhood returns:
I throw him money for more,

supposing he will not make it back
from the bar before falling,

or let him flop out there, frozen,
snuffling at the base of the door.

Now each storm comes reeling round,
tapping wet fingers on windows,
and whining until I lift a glass.

The Quiet Jars

My long-dead Aunt Hazel's house is coming
down—
        she who secured food in translucent
green jars. Looking through one,

I see her print dress slow-swaying across
a cellar of collapsed beams
and swirling dust.
                In another, preserved
peaches squeeze, like ruptured organs, through
cracks in tinted glass.
                        Splinters, not bits of pepper
float between green beans. Her pickles lean
on each other in the only other jar not avalanched
into the debris of corners.
                I had dreaded
the final visit, as if her jars would still be standing,
backed into their shelves, holding their breaths,
                            beribboned
like children for Sunday school.

I'd dreaded the still dust, the hard twist,
the inrush of air, where nothing had changed
for years—
        quiet jars declaring
deliciousness a thing of the past.

Appalachian Gothic

Here's my mashed potato-shaped mother
bending an acre-full of arms
against earth as she punishes the garden.
My bald uncle with the swollen throat
wishes he could swallow life.
In thin blue jeans, he leans upon a hoe.
Here's our house with the frowning
roof that holds back the hills.
The open door yawns out heat.
The sun, sliding out of sight,
overtakes the hill; a thousand slender
clouds snake after it.
Here's our floppy-eared hound smiling
like a clown, his drool dripping
in fat brown puddles in the dirt.
My yellow-young sister sits
pulling bright petals
beside the last broke down step forever.

5.
Some Kind of Pilgrimage

The Mirror

reflects only those dying.
The dead don't come up here
looking for old tax returns.
Unlike the close attic dust,
the dead can't be doubled.

There, I am left-handed and
my hair wants to part right.
Background boxes and broken
lamp look insecure. They
could be thick blobs of dust.

Older than my grandmother,
this glass has her power to
doubt everything. When I
pull the ragged curtain from
the window, the mirror

squints at her Singer in
the corner. "Our machines
are nobler than we are,"
she would say. Her mirror
sews me up in her light.

Skill to Approach the Rose
(For Kathy Miller)

Large and full as a young grandmother
in a red dress, it stands in the corner
of the garden its family has held court in for years.

I only want to go up and sniff,
but I don't have the skill.
Should I have a Sistine Chapel scene
or a Dantean deity in mind?

Instead, my sympathy is for the cells
that have gone to sleep
and have awakened as beauty.
Naked, defensive plaything of my eyes,
it causes me to forget my prison.

It's not love and it's not God.
It's more like a perfect wrist.
I get so close my high school heart blooms.
Yet all my appreciation is not a breeze
that will reach one petal.

Winter Gothic

Out there, in winter darkness, someone's
left a car. Vapors rise
from everything that lives.
The black sides and hood tremble,
as if this machine had been
ridden harder than an Indian pony.
Steam rolls like froth
from the grill. It was forced, according
to the skid marks,
too hard into the turn and melted
at the knees.
The eyes are going out of the headlights.
Squeals linger
in dense air. It would still be screaming,
if looks could speak.
Its chest pours something out now.
Stains melt thin snow
in amber splotches. A tree stands and stares
beside it. Human tracks
walk off, up the road, toward the sky.
Stars continue to spark
in black glass. Its hot heart gives a last
sigh. Snow spins again
just below the hill line. Winter stays
devoted to the rules.

Her Hand on the Chili Bowl

From the door, I notice her.
She moves on her stool,
a bright waterfall
in a large polyester dress.

The counterman says, "Help you, Bud?"
I ignore him past the third stool.
"Hot tea, no cream. Please."
I begin to watch her moves. Something
in the matrix of her picks up on my staring.
I shift to the coat on the rack,
a lavender fuzz, trimmed in lint.

My tea comes; I hover over it
breathing the heat, until I have
an image that she is the housekeeper
of a bankrupt god.
And it has to be her day off.
She's eating a large chili, and it's her day off.
I reach for the sugar and steal
a straight look at her hands. It's
enough to start the romance stirring.
They are fat and round, like peeled potatoes.

Her hand on the chili bowl seems so…
unshielded. Her back and shoulders
are bent, like a bear's, giving in to pleasure.
I love her. The way
she belts down life reaffirms it.

Birds in the Tops of Winter Trees

wait like mourners in the Jewish Cemetery of Charleston.
Two in one tree and one in another almost disappear
as the drizzle thickens against the gray primer of the sky.

Coat collars turned up and heads dark-scarved,
they hunch their shoulders and ruffle their feathers.
The earth is a grave under their gaze.

But this is Appalachia, and they have the sense
that it's something done to them.
Waiting's their invisible strength.

The two fly off in a widening V through diagonal rain,
but the one remaining resists action:
How much food is out there. How much it's needed now.

How far the band will stretch between him and the others.
The names of the dead that drift up like leaves reversing
to trees. The faith that staring will stop the change.

The Dark One

Back from Crossroads Cemetery,
I am a segment of life lying on the couch.
Between my kitchenette and living room,
the quarter-round strip changes green to red

to indicate one room ends here,
another begins there.   I follow the line
with my finger as if it were a distant fence
between farms. Time narrows and enlarges.

Once, I was a few smooth cells,
mother and father in one. Then I divided,
putting in cabinets as I went. After each
funeral, my single life returns:

Rooms round off to doors,
people begin slipping into the earth,
definitions come to an end, radio
songs run to the chorus then start anew.

So Xs of light, from windowsill to table,
cancel noon, purple rises on linked hills.
The *e.pluribus unum* of evening begins.

      (i. m. Ambrosia Williams)

The Wild Ur-Text

The way the frozen grass in November
brushes the soles of my shoes almost clean
isn't wild. Not one blade of grass knows
that we think it is November or that
this was once the ninth month's name.

At twelve, during nightmares,
I knew the werewolves
I conjured after midnight that goose-stepped
through my bedroom
pulling down the shades and eating
the lamps were in my control.
I did not understand the rabbit:
Its soft eyes and feral quickness.

I thought I could think my way to wild,
understanding desire and uncertainty
in the ice-blue eyes of National Geographic
wolves. The hawk in the pupil of the sun,
silent as a black X,
does not know, but is the thing
I sought with the mind's rifle.

I was afraid I might be wild:
The wayward child in me
drove the toy of my body,
forcing the juggernaut
of my car through the fog of eastern
Kentucky last night killing
McDonald's bags, traffic cones,
and that other thing pulling itself
up from the asphalt, in my rearview mirror.

Dawn, I stood at the Monday mirror
whispering to the Saturday in my eyes:
Where's your wild cigar,
your untamed champagne?
Still I have no idea what it means.

At Yeats's Grave

after reading the Brenda Maddox book
that says it may not be his bones lying
here but an amalgam of French paupers',
I wonder whether there is a real Drumcliffe
Cemetery. I cannot bring myself
to lean, silly as any tourist, on
this stone and think I have made some kind of
pilgrimage. I cannot help but wonder
if this is my life at all or just some
collage of minutes spent pursuing the
image of a life, and all that meaning
sought for in art or philosophy were
an opened wreath made to fit whatever
door will take it or horse is forced to lower
its head before the idea of winning.

Undressing Gertrude Stein

I have a dream of taking Gertrude Stein
to a fancy motel in the Catskills.
I pick her up in the restaurant-bar
where lots of newlyweds sit eating
each other with their eyes.
We lounge at the bar laughing

at them and getting drunk.
I get in so close her dark eyes
deepen and her thick cheeks thin.
Her hairline reminds me of Kafka's
and she begins to look Indian. The young
folks start a line dance, so we leave.

In the room, her flannel shirt smells like bourbon.
She is thick and sturdy in the lamplight muted
by my tee shirt. Her white socks,
rolled down to her ankles, pull off easily.
She wears pleated gray slacks and a belt
with a gold horseshoe buckle. Everything
about her is comfortable and warm.

We turn on the radio and dance
like immigrants in our underwear.
With the windows open, the room is nourishing
and cool. My love for her beings
with the way her drab slacks
lie over the chair back beside my jeans
and her formidable bra spreads

on the dresser like two bishops' miters.
But when I see the acne
scars on her back and picture
her school days turning
from the harsh grins and ejaculations
of boys, I fall past where a body
is a body.

Last Night Five Young Owls

came sidestepping onto a high limb
to test their question on the moon,
the river under blue light, and the clouds
that cluttered the hills around the horizon.

Near where I stood about
to pour my cold coffee down the bank,
some bird settling for the night, and perhaps older
than the quintet, heard their choir. I could not think

why he seemed so restless up there,
unless he heard them singing his theme,
the moon's dissolution, the river's disappearance
in air. But I should not see so much in their

question, the hollow night,
the open nest, or glowing dilated eyes.

My Neighbor's Great Maple

I watched its displacement of sky, shadowy in summer;
light green mania in spring; mystical elegance at winter—
snow layering its endless limbs in chiaroscuro light. But
in fall, an obdurate yellow-red explosion against death.

There's enough to cry for these days. I don't want to hate
my neighbor, and I know the big Canadian national emblems
that came waving down from it could poison his swimming pool,
clog all the filters, and stuff the drains. I saw one last October,

a red glove, just touch his baby's chin. She spoke
to it in the tongue that old trees and infants share.
Mrs. Neighbor, pulling up dry ragweed, missed
the new smile and slobbers like syrup.

It could have grown to the base of heaven or the giant's
homeland. The thankless-thing-in-hand snarled
its end and part of mine. Killing it took enough oil and gasoline
to run my Hyundai for a week. Two cranes carried its limbs

to long trucks. My life stands now in stark light.
The clear shale of the sky starts to slide down.
I cannot forgive myself, or him, or come to the stump
with any grace. My heart was bigger in its shadows.

The Exit Sign Over the Body

My father's body lies near the fire door
in the hallway of his apartment building.
He loved jokes, but there's no sign of laughter
in him now. His pouchy cheeks sag hard

toward the runner carpet. His feet inside his black
night watchman's shoes pigeon-toe and his legs
appear to imitate that. He fell without arms up
to shield his fall. How we glow then fade.

I half expect him to roll over and croak, "Gotcha!"
That would be so insensitive he would love it.
Before I go into his living room to call someone,
I do two things no one can see: I hesitate

in his doorway wondering whether he felt the end
coming and came to the hall to let us know
he was leaving for sure, and I look at him again
thinking, "For the first time ever, you are in full
compliance with gravity." That would make him grin.

INDEX OF POEM TITLES

New and Uncollected Poems

After Prayer Meeting, 1959	46
Appalachian Gothic *(New Infinity Review)*	83
Bestiary of Childhood Complaints	34
Boy in the Bath	24
Candlelight	44
Dancing in the Closet	56
Dark Drape	49
Darkness Is for Those Who Can't Stand Shadow *(Green's Magazine* – Canada*)*	58
Dreaming the Ghost	48
Embarrassed by Flowers	33
Floating on Vesuvius Lake	75
Hoarse Voice	23
Identity	26
Ladder to the Sun	42
Long Meal	18
Looking for Life (*The Stinging Fly*)	65
Machine from Animal	37
Martial Arts	54
Mother Sunbathing	59
Nightlight	20
Nostalgia	78
Ode to the Knife in My Ankle	57
One Night	71
Opening Time	17
Outline of Thunder	41
Playground	14
Reunion	67
Shooting at the Moon	36
Singing to the Fan (*Kestrel*)	39
Slug Hunting, 1961	61
Stalking Answers	13
The Bed of Names	22
The Factory of the Body	53
The Hill	27
The Quiet Jars	82

The Unfairness of Flying	45
Tropisms (*Poetry East*)	47
Ugly Fun	72
Uncle Wind	81
Unrequited Everything	79

from
The Bartley Modern Writers Series (1973)

Easy Ride, 1955	25

from
The Courage of Animals (1991)

The Deadly Mantis (*Willow Springs*)	28

from
The Falling Boy (1996)

Boxers' Hands	40

from
Death and the River (1997)

Horses and High Water	31
My Sister's Eye (*Poetry Ireland Review*)	76
The Sadness of Onions	74
The Unnaming, 1958	38

from
Moveable Darkness (2002)

The Boy Who Fell Through Howell's Mill (*Now & Then*)	66
Hunting Spiders at Night in South Point, OH (*The Laurel Review*)	32

from
Greatest Hits—1976-2002 (2003)

Her Hand on the Chili Bowl (*Pulpsmith*)	90
Undressing Gertrude Stein (*New Delta Review*)	95

from
Among Wordless Things (2004)

Model Fire Building (*Poetry in the Park* chapbook)	43
The Mirror	87
Skill to Approach the Rose (*Kentucky Poetry Review*)	88
Winter Gothic	89

from
Birds in the Tops of Winter Trees (2008)

Birds in the Tops of Winter Trees (*Appalachian Journal*)	91
Camping at Greenup Locks and Dam (*The Potomac Review*)	80
The Dark One	92
The First Christmas I Remember (*Poem of the Week – www.salmonpoetry.com*)	16
The Wild Ur-Text (*Wind*)	93

from
Museum Crows (2009)

At Fourteen on the Lake with Grandfather (*Muse Apprentice Guild* – on-line)	62
At Yeats's Grave (*Phantasmagoria*)	94
Beauty Makes a Baby of Me	19
Belief in Soap (*Poetry Northwest*)	15
Last Night Five Young Owls (*The Cortland Review*)	96
My Neighbor's Great Maple (Poet Lore)	97
Playing the Piano (*Motif: Writing by Ear* – anthology)	63
The Exit Sign Over the Body	98

Photograph © Shayne Barker

RON HOUCHIN writes from his home on the Ohio River across from his hometown, Huntington, West Virginia. He taught in public school for thirty years in southernmost Ohio. He has five previous books of poetry, and his work has received notoriety, including Paterson Prize and Pushcart Prize nominations, as well as an Appalachian award for poetry Book-of-the-Year. He travels often to Ireland where his work frequently appears in *Poetry Ireland Review* and *The Stinging Fly*. His poems have been featured in a wide variety of U S venues, such as *Five Points, Birmingham Poetry Review, Valparaiso Poetry Review, Verse Daily, The New Orleans Review, Poetry Northwest, Puerto del Sol, The Southern Poetry Review, Hillbilly Solid* (Radio WMMT) and others. His poems have appeared in Irish and American anthologies: *Dogs Singing: A Tribute Anthology, Salmon: A Journey in Poetry, Motif* I and II, and *We All Live Downstream*. He reads and teaches in writing workshops on both sides of the Atlantic. Salmon published his first book in 1997.